Wind Mountain WITHDRAWN

Also by Fred Chappell

The World Between the Eyes

It Is Time, Lord

The Inkling

Dagon

The Gaudy Place

River

Bloodfire

LOUISIANA STATE UNIVERSITY PRESS

Wind
Mountain A Poem

Fred Chappell

BATON ROUGE AND LONDON 1979

Parts of this poem have previously appeared in these periodicals:
*Appalachian Heritage, Appalachian Journal, Carolina Quarterly, Graffiti,
International Poetry Review, Poetry Miscellany, Quarterly West*, and *Southern
Poetry Review*.

LIBRARY OF CONGRESS CATALOGING IN PUBLICATION DATA

Chappell, Fred, 1936–
   Wind mountain.

   I. Title.
PS3553.H298W5   811'.5'4   79–12332
ISBN 0–8071–0566–X
ISBN 0–8071–0567–8 pbk.

This third volume of Midquest *is dedicated
to the Flowers of this Earth: to Annie and
Kelly, to Candy and Marianne and Sally and
Nickie, to Lee, to Eve, to Mary Lou and Kitty, to Rosamund,
to Gloria, to Anne and June, to Reba and Lillian
and Marlene, to Betty, to Teo, to Mary and Kathleen
and Betsy, to Carol, to Marcia, to Rosemary, to
Doris and Daphne, to Carolyn, to Janis, to Lady
Day, to Gen, to Heather and Bertha, to Noel,
to Lynne, to Louise and Emmy, to oh Lord
each and all, and most of all of course to SUSAN,
you think I'm crazy?*

Io venni in luogo d'ogni luce muto,
che mugghia come fa mar per tempesta
se da contrari venti e combattuto.

Inferno

I came to a place entirely hushed of light,
But rumbling like a tempest out at sea;
The winds fought up and down, this way and that.

Contents

Wind Mountain

◀ Dawn Wind Unlocks the River Sky

Early half-light, dawnwind driving
The trees.
      Wind ravels the scribble of vague clouds,
Fingers the Primavera glass curtain at sill-corner and bellies
It forward, here is my galleon-sail, I can voyage where I whither;
And do not. I push more deeply my face,
Love, to your breast.
Your small breathing harbors me. *Bedroom curls and uncurls with breath*.
Just as the curtain, curling, uncurling, is free to voyage in arabesque,
Not leaving its true place. The small breathing of earth
In our window delivers me the houses and trees, souls aswoon in wind.
Spirits drifting on the dawnwind like sleep-smoke, bonfire
Smoke.
      First sun in the glass curtain dyes it with fire,
                    It is a fire in air,
      It is a fanfare of pure spirit, prelude, aubade.

                                Do I now
Desire you harshly?
No, it is the false desire of fresh morning, my body seeks limit
Merely, curb and margin, wind-plunged.
It is a half-bitter floating in the sea of spirit,

This sea of music,
Passacaglia to every ocean, I am swimming your skin
Of touchless fire and earth-salt. Wind drives me forward like
The spider's doily, anchored at corner and corner and corner to the
Domestic shapes: black hairbrush like a sea urchin, cologne bottle,
Hairpins and comb, deodorant can,
The mirror like a burning window.
                    (Bedroom fills now
              With the aria, Rossini, of blue jay and stinksparrow.)

How the world was formed:
Wind huddled together from every quarter the dead men in it,
Wistful spirits in a gang chained lamenting to the elements,
    Elements carried from the Four Quarters by the East Wind,
By Auster, and Zephyr,
And by rapacious snaketailed Boreas.
Suffering of spirit, suffering of elements,
In one mass.

    My birthday, Year Thirty-Five,
May 28, 1971,
Is tumbling the dawn awkwardly as a broken boxkite, slenderest of tv
Holds it to me, it is Anybody's Birthday, the whole world is born aga
In the morning flush of loosed wind-spirit, exhalation
Of fire-seed and gusty waters and of every dirt, Birthday sails on strea
Of atoms, freshening now the breeze in the Solomons and by Greenla
Brilliantly invading the spicy Virgins.

Fire coming apart now to wind, earth
Divides to rivers, the world of waking shoves me bodyward.
How may I retrieve my spirit where it twirls
In the glasswalled caves of wind? Speech of morning,
Dawnwind driving the trees sunward, it is
Your breath, love, caught back pulsing in your throat where you swir
In the spirit sea, where the inspiration of your bright hair
Flows on the pillow, your bright hair a river
Of fire in early sunlight.
    The pillowslip blood-warm
With breath, the little flame of blood kindles the bedroom.

    I rock now out of the air, out
Of the pure music of absence. In the companioned bed
I retake my body, May 28, 1971.

    Time time time
To rise.
Put your pants on, Birthday Boy, the trees are
Wide awake. The shining net of dream plunges to earth,

Earth rises out of air to greet my flesh.

II   The Highest Wind That Ever Blew :
Homage to Louis

Music is the world over again.

—Schopenhauer

Ever, ever in unanimous voice we drift:
But not you, baby, not you, Satchel-Gator-
Dippermouth. Punch them pepper lead-notes,
Louis. Ride it, fiercemeat, yon and hither.
Birthday morning I put the record on.
Hot Five, hot damn. What a way to never
Grow old! I couldn't count how many times
You saved my life.

                    Tuning my tiny Arvin,
I'd gasp to glimpse through the mindless crackle one gleamiest
Corner of a note you loosed. Once more tell us
About Black Benny and Mary Jack the Bear;
Red-Beans-and-Ricely-Ours, *all ours*,
Let's hear the Good News about Fats Waller.
"You got millions in you and you spend
A nickel": that's what the Message is, okay,
I hear you, shall I ever understand?

What's in that Trumpet is the Tree of Life,
The branches overfreight with canteloupes,
Peacocks, mangoes, and nekkid nekkid women.
And all around the tree a filigree halo
Like a silver lace mantilla. And limb to limb
Zip little silver birds like buckshot dimes,
Kissing and chucking each other under the chin.
Curst be he who worships not this Tree,
Cause you S.O.L., baby   I mean
You   outtaluck . . . It's summertime forever,

Believe to your soul; and this is the River of Jordan.
Everyone was born for a warmer climate
And a jug of wine. You born for it, sweet mama,
And me, and even the blackbox boxback preacher,
He born for it. Up on the Mountain of Wind
I heard in the valley below a lonesome churchbell
Calling home, home, home, home,
And the last swell of the hymn dying at sunset.
Everywhere in your trumpet I heard that.
I'll follow it like a fire in air, I will,
To the purple verge of the world.

                                        Rain aslant the wind
The cozy lovers wind their wounds together.
The weepy eaves peep down into the rooms.
Wind and water drive against the windows
Like a black blind moth in the dark. They sigh
And settle and snuggle. A lemon-colored sun
Warms their innermosts, memory
Of the trumpet-bell uplifted like a sun
Where they'd paid a buck to see the greatest man
Who ever lived, man playing with fire
In air, pursuing his soul in a hovering sun;
Had a tune would melt the polar cap to whiskey.
This dreamshot sun the mellow lovers dream,
It warms them amid each other, the rain goes cozy.

And me too, man, I had me a woman livin
Way   back o' town.
Would wait till the blue-gray smoke of five o'clock
Came down and fetch my bourbon and Beechnut chewing gum
Along the cindery railroad track, counting
The chemical raw smells the paper mill
Dumped into the Pigeon, and the railroad ties.
From tie to tie I whistled *Potatohead Blues*,
Even the clarinet part. It made me happy.
It made me nostalgic for that present moment.

I could have walked like that forever, I could
Have snagged the ballhoot freight to New Orleans
And clung to the windy boxcar singing, *singing*.
I could have lugged my trombone and learned to learn . . .
I learned, anyhow . . . There's something in the woman
More than in the horn to teach you the blues.
Yet still you need the tune, it fixes a pride
On the joy of Traveling Light, there's courage in it.
Father Louis had told me all already.

What's whiskey without the jazz?
Nothin but gutache, nothin to look back on.
Whiskey alone don't fill you that honeysuckle
Sunlight in your vein, it ain't the gin
That makes you shine. It's the man in the cyclone of flame
Who keeps on saying *Yes* with a note that would light
Up the Ice Ages. He's the silver sunrise
In the pit of the body, dawnwind jiving the trees.
Thoreau was right: morning is moral reform,
Gimme a shot. And please play *West End Blues*,
I need to hear the wistful whippoorwill,
To hear the railroad ties hauling the lovers
As they walk down the line, walk down the line
With nineteen bottles of whiskey in each hand,
Going to meet the woman and hear the man.

I've had the warm May nights in the feathery grasses,
Wind poling woozy clouds across the moon,
And the glare light slicing out of the honky-tonk,
Oblong light with a frizzly shape of woman
Troubling its center, one hand on her slouch hip,
Trumpet-flutter in the jukebox behind her
Like a pinwheel of copper fire. She watched the moon.
She too knew that something pulled between them,
The moon and trumpet revolved on a common center
Of gravity which was—where? who? when? how?
Which was *some*where and some*thing*, mystical

But surely palpable, a hungry force
Obtaining as between sharpeyed lovers.

Fire's in the blood, my father told me; wind
Whips it forward, seizing every atomy
In the veins till bloodfire, bloodfire takes the body
Whole, jerks the form of a man along
On that windriver bloodfire, helplessly
A new creature in the Planet of Green Night,
Half funky animal, half pure music,
Meat and spirit drunk together under
The cotton moon. And not one man alone,
Ever, but everyone in reach of the trumpet:
An armada of fireships destroying themselves
To essence pure as wind in the fever nightime.
Papa Louis Armstrong has refashioned us
For our savage reverend assault upon the stars.

III   Second Wind

The day they laid your Grandfather away
Was as hot and still as any I recall.
Not the least little breath of air in hall
Or parlor. A glossy shimmering July day,
And I was tired, so tired I wanted to say,
"Move over, Frank-my-husband, don't hog all
The space there where you are that looks so cool";
But it's a sin to want yourself to die.

And anyhow there was plenty enough to do
To help me fend off thoughts I'd be ashamed
Of later. (Not that ever I'd be blamed.)
The house was full of people who all knew
Us from way back when. Lord knows how
They'd even heard he died. And so it seemed
I owed them to stand firm. I hadn't dreamed
There'd be so terrible many with me now.

I'd fancied, don't you see, we'd be alone.
A couple growing old, until at last
There's one of them who has to go on first,
And then the other's not entirely *one*.
Somehow I'd got it in my mind that none
Of the rest of the world would know. Whichever passed
Away would have the other to keep fast
By, and the final hours would be our own.

It wasn't like that. I suppose it never is.
Dying's just as public as signing a deed.
They've got to testify you're really dead
And haven't merely changed an old address;
And maybe someone marks it down: *One less*.

Because it doesn't matter what you did
Or didn't do, just so they put the lid
On top of someone they think they recognize.

All those people . . . So many faces strained
With the proper strain of trying to look sad.
What did they feel truly? I thought, what could
They feel, wearing their Sunday clothes and fresh-shined
Prayer-meeting shoes? . . . Completely drained,
For thoughts like that to come into my head,
And knowing I'd thought them made me feel twice bad . .
Ninety degrees. And three weeks since it rained.

I went into the kitchen where your mother
And your aunts were frying chicken for the crowd.
I guess I had in mind to help them out,
But then I couldn't. The disheartening weather
Had got into my heart; and not another
Thing on earth seemed worth the doing. The cloud
Of greasy steam in there all sticky glued
My clothes flat to my skin. I feared I'd smother.

I wandered through the house to the bedroom
And sat down on the bed. And then lay back
And closed my eyes. And then sat up. A black
And burning thing shaped like a tomb
Rose up in my mind and spoke in flame
And told me I would never find the pluck
To go on with my life, would come down weak
And crazed and sickly, waiting for my time.

I couldn't bear that . . . Would I ever close
My eyes again? I heard the out-of-tune
Piano in the parlor and knew that soon
Aunt Tildy would crank up singing "Lo, How a Rose
E'er Blooming." —Now I'll admit Aunt Tildy tries,
But hadn't I been tried enough for one
Heartbreaking day? And then the Reverend Dunn
Would speak . . . *A Baptist preacher in my house!*

That was the final straw. I washed my face
And took off all my mourning clothes and dressed
Up in my everyday's, then tiptoed past
The parlor, sneaking like a scaredey mouse
From my own home that seemed no more a place
I'd ever feel at home in. I turned east
And walked out toward the barns. I put my trust
In common things to be more serious.

Barely got out in time. Aunt Tildy's voice
("Rough as a turkey's leg," Frank used to say)
Ran through the walls and through the oily day
Light and followed me. Lord, what a noise!
I walked a little faster toward where the rose
Vine climbed the cowlot fence and looked away
Toward Chambers Cove, out over the corn and hay,
All as still as in a picture pose.

What was I thinking? Nothing nothing nothing.
Nothing I could nicely put a name to.
There's a point in feeling bad that we come to
Where everything is hard as flint: breathing,
Walking, crying even. It's a heathen
Sorrow over us. Whatever we do,
It's nothing nothing nothing. We want to die,
And that's the bitter end of all our loving.

But then I thought I saw at the far end
Of the far cornfield a tiny stir of blade.
I held my breath; then, sure enough, a wade
Of breeze came row to row. One stalk would bend
A little, then another. It was the wind
Came tipping there, swaying the green sad
Leaves so fragile-easy it hardly made
A dimpling I could see in the bottom land.

I waited it seemed like hours. Already I
Felt better, just knowing the wind was free once more,

That something fresh rose out of those fields where
We'd worn off half our lives under the sky
That pressed us to the furrows day by day.
And I knew too the wind was headed here
Where I was standing, a cooling wind as clear
As anything that I might ever know.

It was the breath of life to me, it was
Renewal of spirit such as I could never
Deny and still name myself a believer.
The way a thing is is the way it is
Because it gets reborn; because, *because*
A breath gets in its veins strong as a river
And inches up toward light forever and ever.
As long as wind is, there's no such thing as *Was*.

The wind that turned the fields had reached the rose
Vine now and crossed the lot and brushed my face.
So fresh I couldn't hear Aunt Tildy's voice.
So strong it poured on me the weight of grace.

IV   My Mother Shoots the Breeze

Hot horn hand in my face is all,
The old days. Not that I'm not glad you honor
Daddy and Mama by remembering.
But it wasn't eggs in clover by any means.
To belong like that to Old Times, you belong
To cruelty and misery . . . Oh.
I can't say just what I mean.

Whenever they talk to *you* they leave out hurting.
That's it, everybody hurt. The barns
Would hurt you, rocks in the field would bite like snakes.
And girls have skinny legs, eaten up
By rocks and briars. But I knew always a man
Was looking for me, there was a man would take me
Out of the bottom cornfield for my soul.
My Mama sent me to Carson-Newman College
And the University of Tennessee.
I came back home a schoolmarm, and could watch
Out my first grade windows women chopping
Tobacco, corn, and rocks in the first spring heat.
Two years before, and that was only me
There chopping, but now the pupils said me Yes Mam.
When I read Chaucer they learned to call me Mam.
I'd go back home and milk the cows and grade
A hundred papers. I'd have milked a thousand cows
And graded papers till my eyes went stone
To hear them call me Yes Mam before my Mama.
I taught how to read and write my first grade class
Of six-year-olds and big farm boys and grandmothers.
I'm not humble I was schoolbook proud.

First time I met your Pa he took my slip
Off. "Miss Davis, I want your pretty slip,

If you've got one loose about, for my Science class."
He was going to fly them Benjamin Franklin's kite.
I went to the women's room and squirmed it down
And sneaked it to him in a paper bag.
Under the table at lunch he grinned like a hound.
That afternoon he patched the kite together
And taught them about Electricity.
"Touch that, boys," he said, "if you want a shock.
We've got Miz Silverside's silk panties here."
(Jake Silverside was our Acting Principal.)

But I knew better what I couldn't say
And giggled like a chicken when that kite
Sailed up past my fifth period Spanish window.
I don't know what to tell you how I mean,
But I felt it was me, seeing my slip
Flying up there. It was a childish folly
But it made me warm. I know there's pictures now
Of people doing anything, whatever
Only a doctor could think of, but my slip,
Scented the way that I alone could know,
Flying past the windows made me warm.
J.T.'s the man I want, I thought, *because
He'd do anything . . .* And so he would.

But wouldn't stop . . . Everyday two weeks
In a row he ran that kite up past my window,
Long after he had worn Ben Franklin out.
It's time to show that man that I mean business,
I thought, it's time we both came down to earth.
The very next day I borrowed my daddy's 12 gauge
And smuggled it to school under a raincoat,
And when that kite came past me one more time
I propped and took my time and lagged and sighted
And blew the fool out of it, both barrels.
It floated up and down in a silky snow
Till there was nothing left. I can still remember

Your Pa's mouth open like the arch of a bridge.
"Quit troubling us maiden girls with your silly Science,"
I said, "while we're learning to talk to Mexico."

And one month later, after we were married,
He still called me Annie Mexico.

So. You're the offspring of a shotgun wedding,
But I don't blush about it much. Something
Your father taught me: *Never apologize,*
Never be ashamed, it's only life . . .
And then he was fired for creating life
From alfalfa in a jar on a window sill.

But look, I've told the story that was fun,
And I didn't mean that. What I meant to tell you:
It was hard, hard, hard, hard,
Hard.

V The Autumn Bleat of the
Weathervane Trombone

The Guernseys lift calm brows in the thistly pasture,
What must they think? that some distuneful lovesick
Paramour is moofully wooing? Cows,
Don't sweat it, it's only Fred with his battered sliphorn
Woodshedding a Bach partita on the barn roof.
This edgy October breeze is a freshener,
Don't let it teeter me to lose my toehold,
I'll tumble in the cowlot and bruise my brass.
Johann, thou shouldst be living at this hour,
You'd bust a gusset; if only the Philharmonic
Were here to listen, they'd hire me in a trice.
Is this the way Teagarden started, think you?
He must've started *some*where, so must I,
So must we all.
                    First winter's behind the mountain.

Like the spirit-shapes of great gold plums
The blown tones of the yellow trombone float
Over the fields, their wobble takes on shimmer,
There's something in air in love with rounded notes,
The goldenrod's a-groan at the globèd beauty,
These are the dreams of seeds, aspirations
Of sheeted mica, Ideal Forms of creek-glint,
Sennet and tucket of beech-leaf in its glowing,
Embers of poplar within the sun-warm crowns,
The eyes-in-air of blissful Guernseys, glass eyes
Full of the hands the little yellow hands
Of autumn drifting where they drift in blue,
Blue first-cool, the bluegold music of autumn,
Half sleep, half harmless fire, halved buttermoons,
Bring me my trombone of burning gold, bring me

My harrowing desire, bring me power
To float the cool blue air at the hinge of the year,
These notes not purely born, no, but take
A purity from air and field and sky
As they boat the wind-alleys like happy balloons,
Impure world taking purest shape in the
Bubbles of breath Bach-blown, O those golden
Fermatas, can you see them nudge and brother
The last yellow tomatoes sunning themselves
On the wilted vine, and snuggling down with the pumpkins
And bloodfire bellybloated candyroasters,
The thirty-second notes in tricky clusters
Like bunches of grapes are bunches of blue grapes,
And the chromatic eighth-notes emerge like apples,
Late-sweet streaky slightly flattened apples,
The solid apples that build their nests as high
As ever Earth can reach in the waltzing tip
Of the gnarly witchyfingered ragbark tree,
The tree in the pasture where the Guernseys wait for windfall
Patiently as the Ice Age at the Pole
Because they know an early Boreas
(Rapacious snaketailed) will bring the plunkers down,
O Susan Susan you should've been there when
The cows ate up the apples,
There's nothing quite so *musically* percussive
As the molar gronchle of apple in cow-maw,
And it wasn't was it? only apples they crunched
But some loose sixteenth-notes of J. S. Bach
Mixed in with apples shining in pasture grass,
And let's suppose that now they think this tree
The Tree of Knowledge, they've tasted the apples of music,
Talismans, and shall they ever be the same?
Hell no. They dance all night till the barns come home.

The sun is hatching the world, what new creature
Will emerge? So what, I'm hatching the barn,

I'm your setting hen with the baroquest cluck,
And what new creature will emerge? Aren't barns
The larval stages of dragons, clattery shaleskins?
Before the Fall goes down we everyone
Of us shall be new animals as strange as snow.

Yellow yellow is the color of time. The land
Is bearing itself to rainbow's end, pot
Of gold overfloods the burnt-off delta of summer,
What a dazzle of driftage, what dribble of daft
Storms the skin of the eye, I'm surfeit to bursting,
Have mercy, October, my eyes have eaten all,
I'm rich to the ears, my buttons are each in danger,
O take this table away I've gluttoned on honey,
Honey the heavy gold of time bronze bees
Have hived in the apple belly of the sun
Where all the Hallelujah candles are lit
And the Birthday Boy is momentarily
Expected, is being garnered in like corn.
In the afterlife of Sun I'll meet George Garrett,
The Golden Wiseacre, and what you think he'll tell us,
Uncle Body?—A lie, of course, some furious
Giggly tale of sex & sin & salvation,
We'll laugh our mortality to death, we'll laugh
Our frailty off . . . My fancy anyhow's
That poets after the loud labor of their lives
Are gathered to the sun, they speak in flame
Forever without erasure, they lie a lot,
Where else could all that hot and light come from?
They'll all be there, Adcock and Applewhite,
Whitehead and Tate and Jackson and Watson and Keens,
Morgan, Root, and Cherry, and Godalmighty
The very thought of it makes my ears hammer.
Trapped in a burning eternity with a herd
Of poets, what kind of fate is that for a handsome
Lad like Truly-yours-ole-Fred?

Corkscrewing

The wind, there goes a leaf of tulip poplar,
Saffron mittshape, one poet's been cast from heaven,
It's too much love of earth that draws him thither,
Bondage of toadstool, the sere the yellow leaf
His fate is sealed, he drives to mineral
Where the tree may root him out again,
The flesh the earth is suits me fine, Nirvana
A sterile and joyless blasphemy.
Give me back my blood, there's mud in it.

O yes, Uncle Body, I'll fly with thee to rootlet
And root, we'll swim come spring the tree's resounding
River-trunk, and fan our flashy shape
In green out where the squirrels are whittling toothpicks.
Take corpus after death? I wouldn't mind,
Identity can stuff it but give me Stuff,
This world's longest loaf of dirt's the staff
Of life, O Death come unbaptize me soon,
My grandfather and I never uncovered
The final source of West Fork Pigeon River,
Wonder does it burst from the solid rock
Or comes it blubbering up from the eyes of dead men?
Whichever never mind, we want to see.

Wind-river, river of flesh, spirit-river,
Fever-stream, all these the Ocean of Earth.
Let's disport it, you and I.
Can hardly wait to swim from Singapore
To Hermeneutics and through the Dardanelles
To Transcendentalism, back through the Straits
Of Hegel right on to Greasy Branch close by
Wind Mountain, look out! the perilous Falls
Of Relativity, whew that was close,
Huh-oh now we're utterly becalmed,
The existentialist Dead Sea's a mush
Of murk, help help I'm boring, ah all right,

Here the pure sweet waters of Music open
Upon a picnic wilderness of light.
Around the World in Eighty Tractates aboard
The good ship Wittgenstein, how's that grab you,
Uncle Body? How now? Asleep again,
Old lunker? Never Aquinas rages your blood,
Never up for a sweaty set of Spinoza,
Never wanted to hike with me the slopes
Of stony Heidegger? Come on, we'll pitch
Our tent tonight under the shadow of Plato.
Where's your sense of landscape got to?
If you don't take care, old hoss, Spirit's gonna
Leave you lonesome behind, then where'll you be?

No don't tell me, I never wanted to know.

But the cleanest way to travel would be to ride
One of these untenable trombone tones
Out upon the bluebleached air, forgetless
Air of crystal, steering the golden note
Over the yellowing fields until in tang
It disappears, dream-bubble's silent pop,
And lets us slide the efferevescent atoms
All by ourselves, look Ma I'm flying no hands.
No feets no nothing. Nothing but eyes and taste buds
Skating the Mirror of Blazing Razors, the Eyeball
Of the Clarity of Transcendental Acids,
Lindy would envy our *Spirit of St. Francis*,
We could fly from here to Chuang Hzu's dream.

A Wilson cloud chamber I think it now,
This globe of sunswept blue, this blueblown
Note aloft in its hour of polished silk,
A chamber alert to every Cosmic Ray,
Every sizzle-streak of energy
Indeterminate unreckonable,
Every little tic in the lymph of the world;

For music reflects refracts makes visible
The hail of impulse Nature keeps tossing over
Her shoulder, sprinkle of feckless seed, heat,
Light, ray-quiver, sound, every wealth.
Entropy too keeps coming by, of course,
But nothing here except when the trombone note,
Sighing, deflates like a golden bubblegum.

I've got a slightly different Big Bang theory:
In the beginning was the Trombone—somewhere,
Somehow—and on its own it blew a true
And bluesy A, and here came rolling that note
Through Chaos, vibrato rich and round as a grape
Of Concord, O what a parable note was sounded!,
And us, we innocent children, we kinds of germs
Of music, on the outer skin of that note crawling
In helpless wonderment. And that's our fate,
We've got to tune and turn the music ever.
So I'll straddle the barn and lip the exercises,
Improve my embouchure and wiggle my slide
Till I get a somewhat humaner-looking lover
Than these bored Guernseys. Girls! girls!
Where are you? Don't you hear Fred's lonesome trombone
Mating call from the highest point in the valley?
You wouldn't let the music of this world die.

Would you?

VI   My Father's Hurricane

Like dust cloud over a bombed-out city, my father's
Homemade cigarette smoke above the ruins
Of an April supper. His face, red-weathered, shone through.
When he spoke an edge of gold tooth-cap burned
In his mouth like a star, winking at half his words.

At the little end of the table, my sister and I
Sat alert, as he set down his streaky glass
Of buttermilk. My mother picked her teeth.

"I bet you think that's something," he said, "the wind
That tore the tin roof on the barn. I bet
You think that was some kind of wind."

"Yes sir," I said (with the whole certainty
Of my eleven years), "a pretty hard wind."

"Well, that was nothing. Not much more than a breath
Of fresh air. You should have seen the winds
That came when I was your age, or near about.
They've taken to naming them female names these days,
But this one I remember best they called
Bad Egg. A woman's name just wouldn't name it."

"Bad Egg?"

       He nodded profoundly as a funeral
Home director. "That's right. Bad Egg was what
I think of as a right smart blow,
No slight ruffling of tacked-down tin.
The sky was filled with flocks of roofs, dozens
Of them like squadrons of pilotless airplanes,
Sometimes so many you couldn't even see between.
Little outhouse roofs and roofs of sheds

And great long roofs of tobacco warehouses,
Church steeples plunging along like V-2 rockets,
And hats, toupees, lampshades, and greenhouse roofs.
It even blew your aunt's glass eyeball out.
It blew the lid off a jar of pickles we'd
Been trying to unscrew for fifteen years."

"Aw," I said.

                 "Don't interrupt me, boy,
I am coming to that. Because the roofs
Were only the top layer. Underneath
The roofs the trees came hurtling by, root-ends
First. They looked like flying octopuses
Glued onto frazzly toilet brushes. Oaks
And elms and cedars, peach trees dropping
Peaches—splat!—like big sweet mushy hailstones.
Apples and walnuts coming down like snow.
Below this layer of trees came a fleet of cars:
T-models, Oldsmobiles, and big Mack trucks;
And mixed in with the cars were horses tumbling
And neighing, spread-legged, and foaming at the mouth;
Cows too, churning to solid butter inside.
Beneath the layer of cars a layer of . . . everything.
What Madison County had clutched to its surface
It lost hold of. And here came bales of barbwire,
Water pumps, tobacco setters, cookstoves,
Girdles shucked off squealing ladies, statues
Of Confederate heroes, shotguns, big bunches
Of local politicians still talking of raising
Taxes. You name it, and here it came.
There was a visiting symphony orchestra
At Hot Springs School and they went flashing by,
Fiddling the 'Storm' movement of Beethoven's Sixth.
Following that—infielders prancing like black gnats—
A baseball game about five innings old.
The strangest thing adrift was a Tom Mix movie,

All wrinkled and out of order. Bad Egg
Had ripped the picture off the screen, along
With a greasy cloud of buttered popcorn."

                                        "Wait,"
I said. "I don't understand how you
Could see the other layers with all this stuff
On the bottom."

                        "*I was coming to that,*" he said.
"If it was only a horizontal stream
It wouldn't have been so bad. But inside the main
Were other winds turning every whichway,
Crosswise and cockeyed, and up and down
Like corkscrews. Counterwinds—and mighty powerful.
It was a corkscrew caught me, and up I went;
I thought I'd pull in two. First man I met
Was Reverend Johnson, too busy ducking candlesticks
And hymnals to greet me, though he might have nodded.
And then Miz White, who taught geometry,
Washing by in a gang of obtuse triangles.
And then Bob Brendan, the Republican banker, flailing
Along with his hand in a safety deposit box.
Before I could holler I zipped up to Layer Two,
Bobbing about with Chevrolets and Fords
And Holsteins . . . I'm not bragging, but I'll bet you
I'm the only man who ever rode
An upside-down Buick a hundred miles,
If you call holding on and praying 'riding.'
That was scary, boy, to have a car wreck
Way up in the middle of the air. I shut my eyes . . .
But when I squirted up to Layer Three
I was no better off. This sideways forest
Skimming along looked mighty dark and deep.
For all I knew there could be bears in here,
Or windblown hunters to shoot me by mistake.
Mostly it was the trees—to see come clawing

At me those big root-arms—Ough! I shivered
And shuddered, I'll tell you. Worse than crocodiles:
After I dodged the ripping roots, the tails,
The heavy limbs, came sworping and clattering at me.
I was awfully glad to be leaving Layer Three."

"Wait," I said. "How come the heavy stuff's
On top? Wouldn't the lightest things go highest?"

"Hold your horses," he said, "*I was coming to that*.
Seems like it depended on the amount of surface
An object would present. A rooftop long
And flat would rise and rise, and trees with trunks
And branches. But a bar of soap would tumble
At the bottom, like a pebble in a creek.
Anyhow . . . The Layer of Roofs was worst. Sharp edges
Everywhere, a hundred miles an hour.
Some folks claim to talk about close shaves.
Let them wait till they've been through a tempest
Of giant razor-blades. *Soo-wish, sheee-oosh*!
I stretched out still on the floor of air, thinking
I'd stand a better chance. Blind luck is all
It was, though, pure blind luck. And when I rose
To the Fifth Layer—"

                    "Wait," I said. "What Fifth?
At first you only mentioned four. What Fifth?"

"*I was coming to that*," he said. "The only man
Who ever knew about the Fifth was me.
I never told a soul till now. It seems
That when the hotel roofs blew off, Bad Egg
Sucked a slew of people out of bed.
The whole fifth layer of debris was lovebirds."

"Lovebirds?"

                    "Lovebirds, honeypies, sweethearts—whatever
You want to call them."

      "J.T., you watch yourself,"
My mother interjected.

       "I'm just saying
What I saw," he said. "The boy will want
The truth, and that's the way it was . . . Fifty
Or sixty couples, at least. Some of them
I recognized: Paolo and Francesca,
And Frankie and Johnny, Napoleon
And Josephine; but most I didn't know.
Rolling and sporting in the wind like face cards
From a stag poker deck—"

       "J.T.!" she said.

"(All right.) But what an amazing sight it was!
I started to think all kinds of thoughts . . ."

         "Okay,"
I said. "But how did you get down without
Getting killed?"

       "I was coming to that," he said.
"It was the queerest thing—"

VII   In Parte Ove Non E Che Luca

From Circle One I came to the more narrow
  Second Circle, lightless, lashed, that place
  Resounding with lament of barren sorrow.

And there smack in the doorway sits Minòs,
  Horrible creature, who with an animal snarl,
  Judges whom he clutches so much dross.

I tell you, when the misfortunate soul
  Comes before him, *it confesses each*
  And every sin. The Connoisseur of Hell

Then assigns it to its proper ditch
  In the inferno, counting up however
  Many times round him his tail will reach.

A multitude before him stands forever;
  They come in single file before the bar
  To confess, and then to hear the judge deliver.

"Say you! who come to this Flophouse of Fear,"
  Minòs, setting momentarily
  Aside his duties, so addressed me here:

"Do you know what you are doing? Are you so free?
  Don't let yourself be fooled by the ample doorway."
  My guide told him: "Hush up your hue and cry.

"Where my friend goes you truly have no say;
  His way is willed where Will and Way are one.
  And that is all the explanation due."

And now the notes of lamentation
  Batter my ears, for I have come to the platte
  Of sighs, locale of true perdition.

I came to a place entirely hushed of light,
   But muttering, as at sea we hear a tempest.
   The winds fought up and down, this way and that.

The storm infernal with never any rest
   Still drives the spirits onward with brute force
   Tipsy, and never ceases to molest.

Up they go to the very edge of the Course
   Of Ruin, complaining, lamenting, aghast.
   For them the Word Divine is sheer remorse.

Into this pain the lovers of flesh are thrust,
   All those who gave their human reason over
   To the delicious fever of carnal lust.

There here, here there, yon-hither, lover and lover,
   Hopeless of the comfort of coming together,
   Of satisfaction. In torn air they hover.

As starlings at the onset of cold weather
   Flocking take wing upon the winter sky,
   So here, the human birds all of a feather.

And like the cranes who always make their way
   Flying a single long unbroken line,
   And crying stridently their broken cry,

Shadows were carried toward me on this wind.
   I said, "Master, can you discover
   For me who they are, so driven and blind?"

"The first you see is that notorious lover
   Whom all will readily recall because
   He kissed and told. His name is Casanova,

"The proud Giacomo. But the sturdy laws
   That govern here hold him obedient
   And helpless in this wind without surcease.

"Yet still he's harried on by his penchant
   For conquest, never to be satisfied;
   Always always he wants to, but he can't.

"And there, if you'll observe the other side,
    Flies one who's ordered under the Laws of Iron
    And on the whirlwind must forever slide.

"His noble name is George Gordon, Lord Byron,
    Who with his verses claimed to have seduced
    Two hundred women of Venice and environs.

"Now see to what a state he is reduced!
    When you return to Earth be sure to tell
    The boys, that *he who gooses shall be goosed*.

"The next of those you see in this loud hell
    You'll know for certain," he said. "Without dispute
    The horniest creature alive since Satan fell.

"James Dickey his name, the Poet in the Cowboy Hat,
    Whose greatest fame is propositioning
    Every woman from here to Ararat.

"No one will deny the man can sing;
    But also no one will deny that ever
    And ever he is after that one thing.

"*Deliverance?* His ceaseless thirst for beaver
    May show him sometime what that word implies.
    Some husband with a knife may him de-liver."

"Master, wait!" I said. "I recognize
    From childhood the round form, the red face
    Of Virgil Campbell, one of my father's cronies.

"May I not hear what brought him such disgrace?"
"Of course," he said, "I'll bid him to this place:"

VIII   Three Sheets in the Wind: Virgil Campbell Confesses

Tell you, J.T., the way you see me now,
A solid by God citizen, ain't how
I've been always thought of. There was a time
I lived as raunchy as any wild boy come
Down off the mountain top, guzzling jar
On jar of whiskey, and zooming a souped-up car,
And chasing after women dawn to dawn.
It never came to mind I might slow down,
Or might as well, since there's no way I'd ever
Have it all, that there's a drowning river
Of moon out there and a river of women too.
I wasn't taking good advice, you know—
Not that plenty didn't come my way.
My woman Elsie made sure to have her say
And she'd leagued up with a hardshell Baptist preacher.
Lordy, how I hated to hear that creature
Stand up and witness at my busting head.
Then Elsie'd say again just what he said
Just one more time. It was no sweet cure
For a thirsty flintrock flaming hangover.
I never paid them any serious mind;
You know how it is, there's a kind
Of crazy gets in the blood and nothing but
The worst that can happen will ever get it out.
The worst that can happen never happened to me,
But there was something that came mighty nigh.

This frolic girl that lived up Smathers Hill—
I won't say her name, because she still
Lives there—appeared to be the country sort
Of willing gal you always hear about
And generally never meet. But we'd fall in

Together now and then, and now and then
She'd take a snort if it was offered nice.
And so we horsed around, more or less
Like kids, had us a drink or two and a laugh.
I'd make a pass, and she was hanging tough.
But finally we found ourselves in bed
Together, and I don't think that that's so bad
And awful Jesus will lock the door on you.
Nothing but an itch for something new
And curious, nothing but a sport we giggled
Over when I laid hold of something that jiggled.
Where by God's the harm? You got a friend
Who right-now needs some help, you lend a hand,
Don't you? And never think about it after.
Well, if a woman's lost the man who loved her
And is feeling low, why not pitch in
And give? Every preacher's brimstone bitching
Won't turn my mind on that. —But looky-here,
I might be trying to make myself seem square
And open. To tell the truth, we sneaked around.
That's what was so unpeaceable in my mind.—
We sneaked and thought we were secret as mice;
But Pigeon Forks is a mighty little place,
And two Saturdays hadn't passed before
Elsie found out what we were doing, and more,
A whole lot more, besides. You'd think the tale
Would talk about our diddling, but that wasn't all
By any means. These snuffbrush gossips hear
A story, they fix it up till it's as queer
And messy as the wiring in radios
And sinful as Nevada. Say adios
To anything you know's the truth when those
Old ladies start to twist it by the nose.

But she got enough of the truth to smell
Us out. And planned with that durn preacher they'd tail
Us around until they saw the living sight

Of us having some fun while they were not.
I'll make it short. They caught us plain as day
Light in her bedroom. Before you could say
Jack Robinson they flung the door wide open
And there we were. Halfway between hoping,
Wishing, farting and fainting, I leapt out
The window and ran like a rabbit showing my scut,
Scared enough to run to Cherokee,
And praying that the shooting wouldn't hit me.
Feet don't fail me now. But it wasn't feet
That done me in. The wind lifted a sheet,
A great big white bedsheet, on the backyard
Clothesline into my eyes. I went down hard.
The clothesline caught me under the chin and down
I went, out cold and nekkid on the ground.

From here on in it's awful mortifying
To talk about. In fact, I'd still be lying
If Elsie was still alive to hear . . . When I
Woke up all I could see was a kind of sky,
A wet-white sky that covered me from head
To toe. It came to me that I was dead—
She'd shot my vitals out—and here's the shroud
They buried me in like a cold and clammy cloud.
I fought against it like an animal,
Kicking and clawing, and got nowheres at all.
I hollered till I damn near deefed myself
And thought how I'd do it all different if
I could only live my earthly life again:
I'd be a sweet and silent religious man.

What had happened was, they'd sewed me in,
In one of those wet bedsheets off the line,
Elsie and the preacher. What they'd done
I didn't know then. But that was *their* good fun.

Then: *pow*! Pow pow pow. I took
Some knocks so hard my suffering eyeballs shook.

Pow pow pow. *So this is hell*,
I thought, *and I've deserved it about as well*
As anybody ever. But still it seemed
Unfair, and came on quicker than I'd dreamed.
You think a sinner would get some reprieve,
If only lying a half-hour in his grave.
But no. Immediately they'd hauled me down
And made a marching drum out of my skin.
I was squealing like a little piggy, not
So much from pain as out of fear of what
Was coming next. I dreaded the boiling oil
And the forty hotted pitchforks up my tail.
Go on and laugh, but I am here to tell
You that if there really is a Hell,
Elsie helped plan it. —Because it wasn't God,
But Elsie laying on with a curtain rod.

There's not much left to say. Finally
Her strength gave out, and there she let me lie,
And went off home. And after the awfullest struggle
I got myself unwrapped and crawled, like a bug will
Crawl, out of that wet sheet. There wasn't a scrap
To wear. I went home dressed like a drowned Arab.

I was a sobered feller. Every time
I'd think of another woman there'd come a flame
Rash all over my skin and I'd remember
Having my ass dressed out like sawmill timber.
And the sight of a hanging bedsheet had reminded
Me, and my dick shrunk up till a flea couldn't find it.

"Virgil, your Elsie did you a sight of good,
Made you respectable," my father said.
"Too bad I can't drink with a man on Reform."

"A drink, you say?" he said. "Well, where's the harm?"

IX   Remembering Wind Mountain at Sunset

Off Hurricane Creek where
the heady rattlers even the loggers
abash, out of Sandy
Mush and Big Laurel and
Greasy Branch, off the hacksaw edge of Freeze Land,
those winds huddle in the notch
atop Wind Mountain, where counties Madison
and Buncombe meet but never join.
Hardscrabble Aeolus,
that stir of zephyrs is the sigh of poor
folk screwed in between the rocks up
Meadow Fork and Sugar Camp and Trust, Luck,
Sliding Knob, and Bluff.
A lean wind and a meat-snatcher. Wind
full of hopeless bones.

High on Wind Mountain I heard
from the valley below
the wearied-to-silence lamentation of busted hands,
busted spines, galled mules and horses, last breeze
rubbing the raw board-edge of the corncrib,
whimper of cold green beans in a cube of fat,
the breathing of clay-colored feet unhooked
from iron brogans.
A glinty small miasma
rises off the rocks in the cornfield.
The cowbell dwindles
toward dusk.

I went walking up Chunky Gal
To watch the blackbird whup the owl.

Friend, you who sit where some money is,
I tell you, Sometimes the poor are

poor in spirit, the wind is robbing
them of breath
of life, wind from always Somewhere Else,
directionless unfocused desire,
but driving the young ones like thistle seed
toward Pontiac, Detroit, Cincinnati,
Somewhere, wherever is money,
out of the hills.
Can't make a go
in bloody Madison, too much the rocks
and thickety briars suck the breath of the hand.
Suck the womenfolk to twig-and-twine
limberjacks, suck the puckered houses sad,
tumbly shack by blackberry wilderness
fills to the ridgepole with copperhead
and sawbriar. The abandoned smokehouse
droops, springhouse hoards dead leaves.

I see blackbird fighting the crow
But I know something he don't know.

Over Hunger Cove
the rain-crow keeps conjuring rain
till Shitbritches Creek is flooded, tobacco
drowned this year one more year,
the township of Marshall bets half its poke
and the French Broad takes it
with a murmur of thunder.
Lord, let these sawtooth tops
let me breathe, give me one good stand
of anything but elderbush and milkweed,
I'll keep Mama's Bible dusted off,
I'll try not to murder
for spite nor even for money,
just let that wind hush
its bones a little and not fly so hard
at the barn roof and the
halfbuilt haystack, I'll go to the Singing

on the Mountain with Luramae this
time I swear I will.

Fished up Bear Creek till I was half dead.
Caught a pound of weeds and a hornyhead.

Where you're from's
Hanging Dog, ain't it, boy I knowed
your daddy years back, that was your Uncle
Lige wasn't it lost his arm at
the old Caldwell sawmill, they called him Sawmill
after, took to hunting sang
and medicine root, heard old Lige had died,
is that the truth, I disremember, he
was how old? Hundred and forty-nine
counting nights and hard knocks,
that's what he told me, I'll never forget.
Standing right there by that stove he said it.

If you could eat the wind,
if you could chew it and swallow
it for strength like a windmill.
If anything could be made of this wind in
winter with its scythes of ice when it comes dragging
blue snow over the ridgetops and down
the mountainsides here to the house, finds any
little cranny, wind squirms through the holes
like an army of squirrels.
Go over and sit by the fire, won't
be long till your fingers turn blue again
anyhow. Somehow
I don't have my proper strength
a-winters, been to the doc how many times,
it's a poser to him says he, I told him
Doc I just get down weak as rag soup and
he says, Maybe you need a rest, By God
rest I says, reckon maybe I do,
why don't I lay up here for a while.

I saw blackbird fighting the hawk,
He whupped his hiney with a pokeweed stalk.

And then he says, Now how you
going to pay me? I says, Pay you doc, you'll just
have to garnisheer them Rest Wages.

Two women fighting over a box of snuff,
Lost three tits before they had enough.

First snow like a sulphate powder, bluish,
and up-top the trees like frozen lace, crystal white
against the crystal blue of morning north,
look fragile as tinsel, no wind yet much,
only down the back of your neck now and again to
remind you how long about milking
time it'll come on.
It'll come, everything hurtful will come on.
Here is the place where pain is born.
No salve or balm.
Ever you notice how deep cold the rocks get?
No I mean it, you hoeing round in the field
summertime, hit rocks, sparks
jumping every whichway, come winter
you can beat all day on a rock with a crowbar,
never see spark one, rocks
get froze up deep in the heart is why, told
my oldest boy, No wonder our raggedy
ass is cold, even the goddam rocks
have done give up.

                And if you was to get
a little warm, go in by the cookstove there,
just makes it worse, wind when
you go out peels the feeling-warm right
off, you'll think you've fell
in Spring Creek River, way it goes over you
ice water, but the funny part is, come summer

same wind out of the same place,
feels like it's pouring out of a coalstove,
ain't a breath of soothe in it. Now that's funny.

Maybe the wind like that gets me so low.
Hateful to think of it stepping on my grave
when I'm took off, and then still clawing
you know the apple tree
and the hayfield and the roof of this house,
still clawing
at my young ones after I'm laid safe
out of it. What's the relief in that?
Under the sod you know here'll
come that Freeze Land wind crawling my joints.

Turkey buzzard took old blackbird flying
Like a pissant riding on a dandelion.

Youngish preacherman, heard him
say they ain't no bad without some good
in it somewhere, wanted
to ask him, What's the good in poison oak,
tell me because I can raise twenty solid acres
right in a jiffy, sawbriar too, didn't think
what was the good of this Freeze Land wind, you
know it gets so much inside you, never think
about it being anything, I mean
nothing, just there is all, not anything.
Something you can't see like that you never think.
Like that War in Europe, what'd I know
back here in the stump roots, but they stuck
me over there in the mud
till wild rose and ragweed took my bottom land.

For fighting niggers and hauling loads,
Pulled fifteen months on the county roads.

Friend, you who sit
in the vale of comfort,

consider if you will that there are corners
in this flab land where shale edge
of hunger is chipping out
hearts for weapons, man don't
look from year to year but day by day
alone, suffering of flesh
is whetting the knife edge of spirit in
lower Appalachia, margins
where no one thinks you're his buddy,
don't come driving that big-ass Lincoln
up Hogback Ridge if you like your paint job,
they's some old
bushy boys in here kill a man for
a quarter, eyegod, you seen about that feller
in the papers? I'm not saying
what I've heard about them Henson brothers,
you knowed old man Henson or your daddy did,
him that burned the sheriff
out, had two boys nigh
as lowdown as ever he was, I
don't know what-all I've heard tell.

Up on Wind Mountain there ain't no help.
Blackbird went and killed hisself.

Friend, sit tight on your money,
what you've got, there's a man
on a mountain thinks he needs it worse.

All this I heard in the stir
of wind-quarrel in Wind Mountain notch,
rich tatters of speech
of poor folk drifting like bright Monarchs.
And then on the breeze a cowbell,
and the kitchen lights went on in the valley below,
and a lonesome churchbell
calling
home, home, home, home

till I could bear it no more.
Turned my back.
Walked down the mountain's other side.

They hauled old blackbird's carcass away,
Buried him head-down-deep in red clay.

Here comes the preacher to say the last word:
"It's a fitten end for old blackbird."

X Hallowind

Setting: Halloween, 1961; Durham, N.C.
Personae: Reynolds Price, Susan, Fred, the rain, the wind

Fred
Listen to it skirl the roof
And tear the ragged eaves as if
The world outside weren't room enough!

Reynolds
Voices.

Fred
What do they say?

Reynolds
"In, in."
The ghosts of stories not yet written
Lisp and whimper like dead men.
It's up to us to chronicle
Their thoughts, that death not treat them all
The way that life did, flat forgetful.

Fred
What a swarm of stories there
Must be, to overload the air
With voices as loud as a river's roar.

Reynolds
The number, of course, is infinite.

Fred
Why couldn't a single story tell it
All?

Reynolds
Ah, that's the helpless poet
In you, the need to generalize
From yours to all men's destinies.

For fiction, those are pompous lies
Which try to stretch the single stories
Into laws akin to physical laws.

Fred

You're no one to talk. *A Long
And Happy Life* will make as strong
An example as any poet's song.
What is it but the ancient tale
Of Cupid and muddled Psyche? All
That's added is the motorcycle.

Reynolds

That's not the way I see it. These
Are Warren County sweethearts whose
Lives shape local clarities.

Fred

Suppose, though, that I choose to read
The myth within it. Is it so bad
To add more meaning to each word?

Reynolds

But do you add or take away?
A certain lake, a certain tree,
A particular girl on a certain day—
A fleeting tang in Carolina . . .
You'd give that up for some diviner
Heavy symbol?

Fred

                    But if I find a
Paradigm as old as fiction
Itself conformably mixed in?

Reynolds

Well, that requires some hard reflection.
If you think it's there it's there,
I guess. It could be anywhere,

Or not at all. *Things as they are*:
That's the novelist's true belief.
I regard the "symbol" as a thief
Which steals the best parts of a life.

Fred
I think I don't believe you quite.

Reynolds
I'm overstating it a bit
To make my point. Jim Applewhite
Would have conniptions if he were here—

Fred
And Spender too.

Reynolds
—*Things as they are*:
I'll stand by what I see and hear.

Fred
And does that mean the poet's blind
And deaf? Let's say he's trained his mind
To hear all, multivoiced as wind.

Reynolds
Wind's what the poet cannot fix;
The current of life from Eden to Styx
Demands an accounting of *the facts*.
Poems are maimed by their timelessness,
Lack of distinction in *was* and *is*,
That stony stillness like a star of ice.
The *symbol* is at last inhuman,
A cruel geometry, and no man
Ever loved one like a woman
Or a novel.

Fred
Oh, come now. Yeats—

Reynolds
I except of course the crazy poets
Who can fall in love with rocks and he-goats.

(*Enter Susan with tea and cakes.*)

Fred
Now just a minute—

Susan
         Boys, boys.
I'm surprised you make such a dreadful noise.
—Reynolds, your Oxonian poise!
Old Fred *never* had a grain
Of couth, but you're a *gentleman* . . .
Don't you-all hear how the wind's brought rain?

(*They fall silent and listen. Susan pours.*)

Fred
The most symbolic line there is,
And fullest of hard realities,
Is Shakespearean: "Exeunt omnes."

Reynolds
Your poet's a foe to love and laughter.
Here's the line one gives one's life for:
"They all lived happily ever after."

Susan
I wish I weren't a writer's wife.
I'd live as harmless as a leaf
And cuddle up in a dear warm life.

The Rain (to The Wind)
What say we work us up some brio
And drown this silly wayward trio?
My favorite line is "Ex Nihilo."

The Wind

Leave them in peace, if peace there is
For their clamorous little species;
Let them relish their flimsy wishes.
Tomorrow and tomorrow we
Advance against them frightfully.
This night at least they have their say
Together; and the force of Time
Upon their arts, upon slant rhyme
And paragraph, delays for them.
It's soon enough that we dissolve
Their names to dust, unmoving move
Against their animal powers to love
And weep and fear. It's all too soon
They grow as silent as the moon
And lie in earth as naked bone.
We'll let them sit and sip their tea
Till midnight; then I'll shake the tree
Outside their window, and drive the sea
Upon the land, the mountain toward the Pole,
The desert upon the glacier. And all
They ever knew or hoped will fall
To ash . . . Till then, though, let them speak
And lighten the long dim heartache,
And trifle, for sweet trifling's sake.

XI   Wind Subsides on the Earth Riv

Every water is asleep.

The wind only
Gentles the earth to breathing, to body of breath, it is
This wind from the tips of mountains and from hollers,
Saying, *Home, home,*
Earth is home. Where have we not drifted in fire,
In water, in air?
                    But Earth is the mouths of wind.

My sister wind, wind my mother,
You my confusion of fingers,
I know I shift this world an injured air,
I know how I am guilty in too much space,
And how the churchbell lifts its somber redundance.
The churchbell says:
Home, home   home to the animals,
                            home to the crouchings and lickings, ho
                            to twilight, to the small coals of old fire.

Susan, have I not loved you?
This world is wind, and homeless.
Here now I lay my stone of fire, crying,
Touch me, touch, I cannot come apart from the wind.

I come apart from the wind, crying,
Touch me, bright river, your sleeping
Makes this earth domestic.

                        Wind, it is the last thing
On Earth, kissing the petrified rubble of dream.
I dream, Susan, we are not wind;
I dream we are the breath and flame of the last fire that lived.
Earth huddles to our hands,

                         hands coming apart now
To water, hands luckless in earth, this earth
With its mouths of wind coming apart to mind,
Mind drifting to fire, to water, no bodies,
What can we love with?
We cannot love with wind, tell me, Estuary,
We are but both and each.

The wind in the meat night says,
You have no hands, no bodies, you cannot speak.
Our figures
Collide touchless as reflections of Buicks in supermarket windows.
Ghost and no ghost,
I lift you toward that profound atom,
Earth,
I know you dream of.

We have lived to die.
We have lived at last to kiss
Our forefathers
With our green earthlips.

                         Wind
Wind wind
Says, We shall ever.

It does not end like this, wind taking
The last fever of water.
There is a final shore.
In the winds of rocks my blood shall learn to dance.

Susan Susan   this broken tide